Coral Snake

By Jamie Honders

Gareth Stevens
Publishing

Please visit our website, www.garethstevens.com. For a free color catalog of all our high-quality books, call toll free 1-800-542-2595 or fax 1-877-542-2596.

Library of Congress Cataloging-in-Publication Data

Honders, Jamie.
Coral snake / Jamie Honders.
    p. cm. — (Killer snakes)
Includes index.
ISBN 978-1-4339-5634-8 (pbk.)
ISBN 978-1-4339-5635-5 (6-pack)
ISBN 978-1-4339-5632-4 (library binding)
1. Coral snakes—Juvenile literature. I. Title.
QL666.O64H66 2011
597.96'44—dc22

2010047689

First Edition

Published in 2012 by
Gareth Stevens Publishing
111 East 14th Street, Suite 349
New York, NY 10003

Copyright © 2012 Gareth Stevens Publishing

Designer: Michael J. Flynn
Editor: Greg Roza

Photo credits: Cover, pp. 1, 15, 17 Michael & Patricia Fogden/Minden Pictures/Getty Images; (pp. 2-4, 6, 8, 10, 12, 14, 16, 18, 20-24 snake skin texture), p. 7 (kingsnake) Shutterstock.com; p. 5 Jim Merli/ Visuals Unlimited/Getty Images; p. 7 (coral snake) Joe McDonald/Visuals Unlimited/Getty Images; p. 9 (eastern coral snake) iStockphoto.com; p. 9 (Arizona coral snake) Gerold & Cynthia Merker/ Visuals Unlimited/Getty Images; p. 11 William Weber/Visuals Unlimited/Getty Images; p. 13 Charles Melton/Visuals Unlimited/Getty Images; pp. 18-19 Gary Meszaros/Visuals Unlimited/ Getty Images; p. 21 Michael Fogden/Photolibrary/Getty Images.

Printed in the United States of America

CPSIA compliance information: Batch #CS11GS: For further information contact Gareth Stevens, New York, New York at 1-800-542-2595.

Contents

Boldface words appear in the glossary.

Colorful but Deadly

A coral snake is a colorful but deadly animal. It makes **venom** inside its body. The coral snake uses its **fangs** to shoot the venom into its **prey**. The venom is strong enough to kill!

Red on Yellow

Most coral snakes have black, red, and yellow bands. Many nonvenomous snakes look almost the same as the coral snake. However, only the coral snake has wide red bands between thin yellow bands.

king snake

coral snake

7

Coral Snakes in the Unites States

Coral snakes live all over the world. They like warm areas with lots of hiding places. There are two main types of coral snakes in the United States. They are the eastern coral snake and the Arizona coral snake.

Arizona coral snake

eastern coral snake

Adult eastern coral snakes are about 20 to 30 inches (51 to 76 cm) long. The yellow bands on this snake are often thin and dull. Some don't have yellow bands the full length of their bodies. They live in wooded, sandy, and **marshy** areas. Most are found in Florida.

eastern coral snake

11

Arizona coral snakes are shorter and thinner than eastern coral snakes. Adults are only about 13 to 21 inches (33 to 53 cm) long. They often have brighter yellow bands than eastern coral snakes. Sometimes the bands are white instead of yellow. Arizona coral snakes like hot, dry, rocky areas.

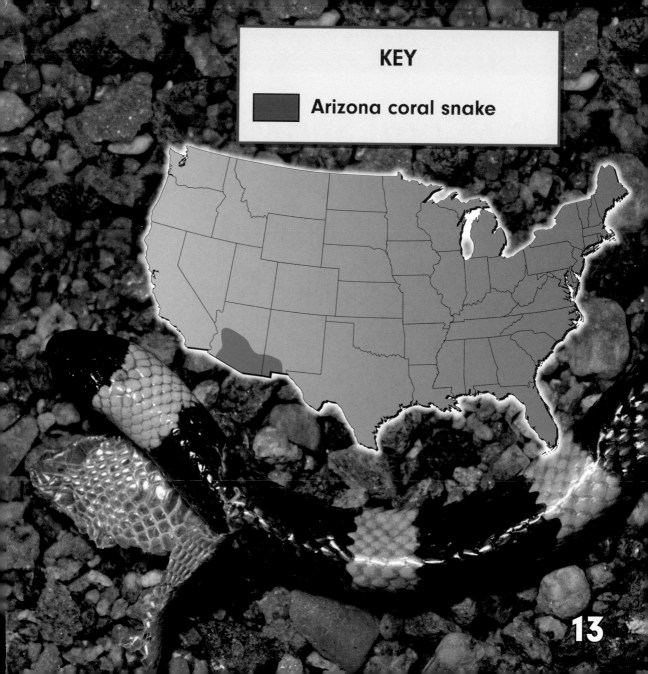

Baby Coral Snakes

Female coral snakes lay 2 to 13 eggs in summer. Then they leave the eggs. The babies break out of the eggs in 2 to 3 months. They are about 7 inches (18 cm) long. Baby coral snakes are fully venomous. They start hunting for food right away.

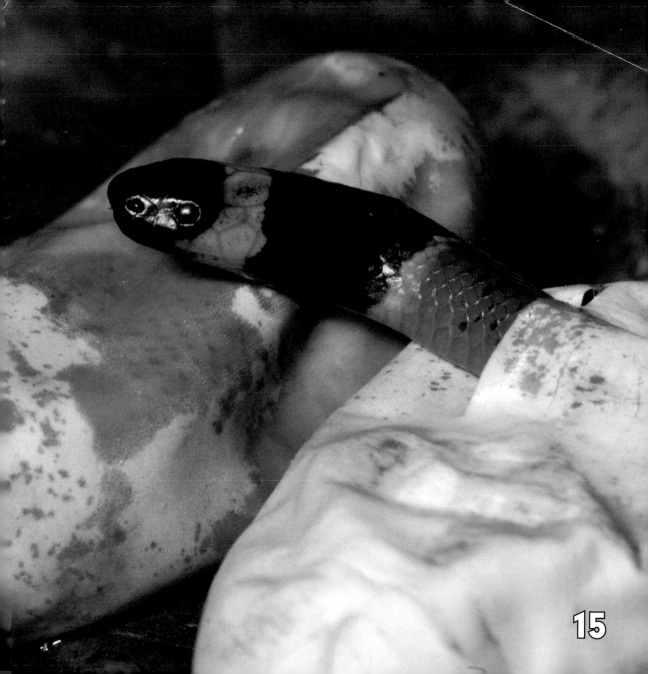

15

On the Hunt

Coral snakes eat lizards, frogs, mice, and other snakes. They hide in leaves and surprise their prey. Like other snakes, coral snakes use their tongues to smell for food. Once a coral snake bites its prey, it doesn't let go until the animal is dead.

17

Coral Snake Venom

Coral snake venom is nearly as strong as cobra venom. However, the coral snake is much smaller than a cobra. Because of this, a coral snake bite is less deadly. The venom is still strong enough to kill or **stun** small animals.

People and Coral Snakes

Most coral snake bites happen when people step on them. A person who has been bitten by a coral snake needs to take a **medicine** called antivenin. Because of antivenin, no one in the United States has died from a coral snake bite in many years.

Snake Facts
Eastern Coral Snake

Length	about 20 to 30 inches (51 to 76 cm)
Colors	black, red, and yellow bands
Where It Lives	southeastern United States
Life Span	up to 7 years
Killer Fact	Coral snakes have small mouths and short fangs. It's harder for them to shoot venom into prey than it is for other snakes. To make up for this, coral snakes often chew on their prey instead of just biting them!

Glossary

fang: a long, pointed tooth

marshy: wet, soft, and muddy

medicine: a drug taken to make a sick person well

prey: an animal hunted by other animals for food

stun: to shock something so it can't move

venom: something a snake makes inside its body that can harm other animals

For More Information

Books

Sexton, Colleen. *Coral Snakes.* Minneapolis, MN: Bellwether Media, 2010.

White, Nancy. *Coral Snakes: Beware the Colors!* New York, NY: Bearport Publishing, 2009.

Websites

Eastern Coral Snake

animals.nationalgeographic.com/animals/reptiles/eastern-coral-snake/

Read more about the eastern coral snake.

Western Coral Snake

www.desertusa.com/mag98/may/papr/du_westcoral.html

Read more about the western (Arizona) coral snake.

Index